Imagine What I'll Be When I Grow Up

By

Vinesha McIntosh

Written by Vinesha McIntosh

Illustrations by Canva Pro

For information regarding permissions and/or other, please email

legacybookcollection@gmail.com

Paperback: ISBN 978-1-7388179-0-0

EBook : ISBN 978-1-7388179-1-7

This book is dedicated to my three sons
Macai, Levi and Josai.

This book belongs to

____

I want to be a(n) ______________________________

when I grow up.

Date:______________________

"I think, I'll be an astronaut."
"I will help to make new discoveries in space
one mission at a time!"

"Or maybe, I'll be a Youtuber?" "Yes!" "I will make funny videos so my friends can like, subscribe, and share my channel."

" I know, hmmm?" I'll be a doctor."
 "I will make sick people better and
happier."

" I love soccer." "So I'll become a famous soccer star!"

"I will play for my team and country on the world's biggest stages."

Today is
Monday, December 19, 2022

"I'll be a teacher, now that should be fun!" "I will teach my kids their ABCs, 123s, and to sing DOH-RAY-ME!"

You are smart, you are brave
and you are loved

BREAKING
LIVE
NEWS

"Maybe I'll be a news reporter."

"I will bring you breaking news and all you need to know about your day."

"I'll be a dancer." "And who knows, I will perhaps be dancing with the stars in Hollywood."

"I'll be an accountant". "All I know is that they get real busy during tax season." "So I think, that makes them SUPER important!"

IN GOD WE TRUST

"I'll be a high court judge."
"I promise that I will rule with fairness and good sense." "I pinky promise!"

SOLD

"I've seen this one on tv." "Maybe, I'll be a realtor." "I will help families find their forever home."

"I'll likely be an architect, because of my awesome drawing skills! "I will design one building after another."

"There are so many AMAZING things I could become!"

"With effort, I can become anything I wish to be.""I have plenty of time to decide because I'm still so little.

Thank you for your purchase!

Please like Legacy Book Collection on Facebook to receive updates on new publications that will be released in 2023.

When your little reader has signed the "this book belongs to" page, please post a photo of it on our page. We would love to see it so that we could encourage them!

We truly hope that you will like this book and that it will become a family favorite. Please leave a review so that other families can join the fun.

Many Thanks.

About The Author

Vinesha was born in Kingston, Jamaica. She migrated to Canada in 2014 and now lives with her family in Kelowna, British Columbia. She is a wife and mom of three vibrant, entertaining boys.

She has a heart for Christ and finds inspiration in her daily experiences as she supports her husband and raises her children.

Helping others, healthy marriages, and children are among her interests. She wants to see them reach their full potential and live lives of meaning and fulfilment.

Made in the USA
Columbia, SC
20 December 2023